STUDY GUIDE

for

SENDERS

How your church can identify, train,
& deploy missionaries

PAUL SEGER

STUDY GUIDE

for

SENDERS

How your church can identify, train, & deploy missionaries

Copyright © 2015 Paul Seger
All rights reserved.

All rights reserved solely by the author. No part of this book may be reproduced in any form without the permission of the author except in the case of brief quotations in critical articles or reviews.

Cover, book layout & graphic design by
Jjinc Design | Canton GA | jjincdesign.com

Published by Sawubona Press

ISBN-13: **978-1517154110**
ISBN-10: **1517154111**

How to use this Study Guide

This guide is designed to be used in a group setting with opportunity for interaction. The group should be the designated team within the local church that has responsibility to design and drive the missions endeavors. They should have some decision-making authority or have a direct channel to the decision makers of the church so that ideas can be implemented.

It would be helpful for each participant to have a copy of the book *Senders* and a copy of this study guide. I recommend that you schedule 10 sessions that are 60 to 90 minutes long so that there is ample opportunity to wrestle with the content of the book and make practical application. Before each session, participants should read the appropriate chapter and make provisional observations in the study guide.

During the group meeting there should be freewheeling discussion with an attempt to come to a consensus on the position of the group on the questions and topics at hand. There may be two options:

1. The group may quickly agree to the answer and position of the church.
2. Some issues may be too complex to conclude in a 90-minute session. The group may assign a smaller team or an individual to do further research or thinking on a topic to report back to the group at a later time.

If your group will work through all of the questions and topics in the study guide, it will produce a basic philosophy and strategy for Great Commission ministries for your church. It would be helpful to have someone gather all of this information into a singular document. This strategy statement should include the following elements for each action point:
1. A description of what will be done
2. A designated person who will be responsible to see that it is done
3. A due date for which that person will report back that it has been accomplished. If it is on an ongoing assignment, it is helpful to specify the dates that this individual will report on the consistency and progress of implementation.

STRATEGY	PERSON RESPONSIBLE	DATE

CONTENTS

How to use this Study Guide iv

1. Why Bother? 2

2. At What Price? 6

3. Ground Zero 10

4. You're It 16

5. Training 20

6. Go Do What? 24

7. Agencies 26

8. Money 30

9. Prayer 32

10. Staying Home 34

Conclusion 38

Appendix A
Outcome Objectives for an Equipped Leader 42

Outcome Objectives for a Leading Lady 54

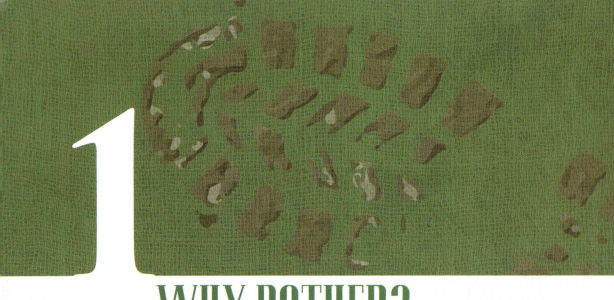

1 WHY BOTHER?

This is a foundational chapter that is at the core of everything else related to Great Commission ministries. Unless there is clarity and a firm commitment to the ideas in this chapter, there will be confusion and conflict later on. These issues may seem theoretical, but they are critical to establishing a missions strategy.

A. What is your group answer and argument for the question: "Are the heathen really lost?"

   ....
   ....
   ....

B. What is the level of the church's commitment to missions?

   Not a priority at all   All-consuming priority

   ← 0   1   2   3   4   5   6   7   8   9   10 →

C. Write a position statement for your church on compassion ministries and social justice.

....
....
....
....
....

D. Decide if social justice and compassion should be part of your missions strategy and budget. If so, what will that look like? If not, what will the church do with regards to this topic?

....
....
....
....
....

there is a difference between the Great Commission and the Great Command

BMW Position Statement on Compassion Ministry

Biblical Ministries Worldwide affirms the biblical truth that we serve a God of compassion (Ex. 34:6; Ps. 86:15, 103:13, 145:8-9; Lam. 3:22-23; 2 Cor. 1:3; James 5:11), an attribute He shares with humankind (Gen. 43:30; Col. 3:12; 1 Jn. 3:17-18).

- Compassion is one of the themes of Scripture, and one of the motivations for our Savior's sacrifice for us (Mt. 9:36; 14:14; 20:34; Mk. 1:41; 6:34).
- Compassion ministry was commanded throughout the Law of God (Ex. 22:21-27; Deut. 14:28-29, 24:17-22), and it was a sign of true repentance and revival in Scripture (Is. 1:16-18; Jer. 7:5-7, 22:3-5; Zech. 7:9-12).
- In the New Testament, the ministries of Christ, the Apostles, and the early church intertwined the three elements of the gospel message, ethical teachings, and compassion ministry into a unified gospel ministry (Mt. 4:23, 9:35-36, 18:21-35, 25:31-46; Luke 7:22, 10:30-37, 15:11-32; Acts 3:1-10, 4:36-37, 5:12-16, 5:42-6:7, 8:4-13; Gal. 2:10, 6:10; James 1:27, 2:15-17; Rom. 12:13, 15, 20; Eph. 2:10; Tit. 3:8, 14).
- Compassion is commanded, it is an element of godliness and Christlikeness, it is portrayed as pure and undefiled religion, and it will be part of the basis of future judgment. (James 1:27; 2:5-10; 5:1-6)

BMW missionaries should be committed to a life of compassion, combining practical help, the gospel message, and ethical teachings for the lives of the needy around us, both believers and nonbelievers.

At the same time, BMW missionaries must consistently resist any attempt within so-called Christendom to redefine sin in terms of physical, social, or economic human suffering, to redefine ministry as social work, or to redefine the work of Christ, the gospel, or salvation in terms of merely improving the human social condition.

The **gospel message** is of primary importance when engaging nonbelievers: it was Jesus' primary reason for coming to earth (Mk. 1:38), it was the center of the Great Commission (Mt. 28:19-20), it was the focus of the Apostles (1 Cor. 9:16-23), and it is the power of God in changing the eternal destiny of a human being (Rom. 1:16-17). The gospel message, therefore, is central, theological, objective, and individual.

The **gospel message** includes the message but also involves practical, relational, interactive and culturally sensitive labor and teaching directed at the whole person to help restore and transform the four broken human relationships with God, self, others, and the creation (Gen. 3:6-24; Luke 4:18-21).

BMW missionaries desiring a compassion ministry should educate themselves and make every effort to help relieve the suffering in their communities using great wisdom and a keen sensitivity to the will of the Lord, so that they do not hurt themselves or those they are trying to help. Those who engage the poor and suffering should, without neglecting the gospel message and gospel ministry defined above:

- ideally adapt themselves to identify with their host society: living near or among the target recipients, continuously studying their culture, worldviews, history, and language, connecting with them in ways that are in harmony with the moral and ethical teachings of Christ, and communicating God's truth (Acts 17:18-34; 1 Cor. 9:19-23);

- understand the biblical causes of poverty and clearly recognize the differences between assisting in relief, rehabilitation, and development situations (Ex. 22:25; Prov. 19:17, 22:9; Acts 11:29-30);

- take care to avoid paternalism and the reinforcement of third-world stereotypes in their words and actions (Ex. 23:6, 11; Prov. 14:20-21, 16:19, 17:5, 22:7; James 2:1-7);

- advise and adhere to proper stewardship principles on their team and on short-term teams that are looking to assist with compassion ministry; and

- aim to involve those who are suffering with the remedies for their own condition so that they, in turn, can minister to others (2 Cor. 8:2; Eph. 4:28; 2 Thess. 3:6-12).

2. AT WHAT PRICE?

Jesus made it very clear that before heading into an endeavor, it is wise to first count the cost (Luke 14:25-33). The following exercises will help you determine whether your church is willing to pay the price to identify, train, and send your own missionaries. It is designed to help the group unify around a commitment to specific goals and strategies to fulfill the Great Commission.

A. Discuss your attitudes toward the high cost of supporting a missionary. What are your conclusions?

   ....
   ....
   ....
   ....
   ....
   ....
   ....
   ....

B. Write one sentence that describes the kind of person you would like to send as a missionary.

....
....
....

PRESENT REALITY	FUTURE GOAL
We presently designate ___ % of the church's overall budget for missions	In the future, we would like to designate ___% of the church's overall budget for missions
We presently support missionaries an average of $____ per month (or ____% of their support needs)	In the future we would like to support missionaries an average of $___ per month (or ____% of their support needs)
We presently support a missionary who is a member of our church an average of $____ per month	In the future we would like to support a missionary who is a member of our church an average of $____ per month

C. What is your church's position on supporting Nationals?

....
....
....
....
....

D. What is your strategy for honoring and supporting the parents of missionaries?

   1. ....

   2. ....

   3. ....

   4. ....

   5. ....

   6. ....

   7. ....

   8. ....

   9. ....

   10. ....

determine if your church is willing to pay the price to identify, train and send your own missionaries

3
GROUND ZERO

It is critical for the church to embrace the concept that a mission emanates from the local church. While institutions like colleges and mission agencies may assist in the process, the central agent for fulfilling the Great Commission is your assembly. This session will assist you in evaluating and aligning your local church with its central purpose statement.

A. What is the mission statement of your church?

    ....

    ....

    ....

    ___ Are you pleased with the way this is stated?

    ___ Does it include the Great Commission?

    ___ Is it short enough for all members to memorize?

    ___ Is it clear using words that people understand?

B. Diagnostic: Do your church activities directly contribute to the fulfillment of your mission statement? List everything on the church calendar and evaluate whether it directly impacts your mission (e.g. worship services, Sunday school, youth program, VBS, prayer meetings, small groups, fellowship dinners.)

ACTIVITY OR PROGRAM	YES - NO

the central agent for fulfilling the Great Commission is your assembly

GROUND ZERO | 11

C. Fill in this chart and evaluate your church's present fulfillment of Acts 1:8. What would you like to see changed in this chart within the next five years?

ACTS 1:8 IMPACT	JERUSALEM (City)	JUDEA (State/Country)	SAMARIA (Cross-Cultural)	UTTERMOST (World)
What activities of the church impact each of these areas?				
How much money is the church budgeting toward each area?				
How much prayer is focused on each area?				
What training is available to equip people to minister in each area?				
How many people are involved in each area of ministry?				
What evidence is there that God is blessing the efforts of the church?				

D. Evaluate your leaders. When it comes to the Great Commission do they regularly:
   ___ Pray publicly for God to raise up missionaries?
   ___ Preach on the subject of missions?
   ___ Pester the congregation about "the" mission?
   ___ Poke some in the ribs that ought to consider becoming missionaries?

E. What are some vital signs that might indicate the missions health of your church?

....
....
....
....
....
....
....

F. Training checklist

COMMIT: Is there a commitment to make leadership training a priority even if it means canceling some of the existing programs?

....

DEFINE: Describe in one sentence what an equipped leader looks like.

....
....
....

IDENTIFY potential leaders in your church who have the primary qualification of faithfulness who could be your next generation of leaders.

....
....
....
....
....

ARTICULATE how your church will train missionaries.

. . . .
. . . .
. . . .
. . . .
. . . .

CHOOSE resources for training.

. . . .
. . . .
. . . .
. . . .
. . . .

CREATE a learning environment with the existing leadership modeling life-long-learning. What is your strategy to do this?

. . . .
. . . .
. . . .
. . . .
. . . .

*articulate how your
church will train missionaries*

4 YOU'RE IT!

The local church must assume its role of recruiting missionaries. It must decide whether to wait for volunteers or be proactive in training leaders and identifying missionaries. It must have a practical pathway that begins in the nursery of the church and ends on the mission fields of the world. People need to see how you get there. This session will help to crystalize some of those ideas for your congregation.

A. What is the group's commitment level to the idea that the local church is the primary recruiting ground for missionaries?

B. What is the group's commitment level to the idea that the each church member has a responsibility for recruiting missionaries?

C. What level of leadership experience should a person have in your church before you send them to the mission field? Would you agree to send a young person like Timothy to be mentored on the field by experienced missionaries?

....

....

....

D. What will your church do to assure regular, fervent prayer that God will raise up missionaries from the congregation?

....
....
....
....
....
....
....

E. What are the minimal personal qualifications to be a missionary sent from your church?

....
....
....
....
....
....
....

F. How does your church understand the concept of the "call." If someone indicates they want to be a missionary, what would you expect to see in them that would indicate God is in this and that your church should send them to the mission field?

....
....
....
....
....
....
....

G. How will you communicate the concepts of this chapter to the congregation in an ongoing basis?

....
....
....
....
....
....
....
....
....
....
....

be proactive in training leaders and identifying missionaries

5 TRAINING

The presupposition of this chapter is that the local church has the responsibility of training missionaries. It may outsource some of this to colleges and agencies, but ultimately it is the responsibility of the local church to make sure it is done. This session will help you identify how this will happen in your congregation.

A. EVALUATE:
   ___ How many missionaries does your church support for which you are their **Sending** church?
   ___ How many missionaries does your church support for which you are their **Supporting** church?
   ___ What would you like to see as a ratio of missionaries that view your church as a sending church vs. a supporting church?

B. List the criteria that are important to your church when choosing to be a supporting church for a missionary from another church.

   . . . .
   . . . .
   . . . .

....
....
....
....
....
....
....
....
....
....

C. What obstacles exist that keep your pastor from devoting a large part of his time to training leaders?

....
....
....
....
....
....
....

D. Design a farm team system for your church that will provide a clear path for any 10-year-old in your church to see how he or she could become a missionary from your church.

E. To be sent as a missionary from your church, what does a person need to:

KNOW	BE	DO

F. Which of the above qualifications will your church outsource to someone else to train a church member and which qualifications will your local church train?

....
....
....

identify how training missionaries will happen in your congregation

TRAINING | 23

6

GO DO WHAT?

If your church is going to send a missionary, there should be no ambiguity about what they are supposed to do once they get there. Since every ministry setting is so different, the church cannot micro-manage how the missionary should do his job but the church should know exactly what success looks like. The church should then release the missionary to determine the best way to get to the goal. This session will help a church determine who should do what by when.

A. Imagine you are having the commissioning service to send a missionary from your church. The pastor stands up and gives a charge to the couple and tells them what they should accomplish while they are gone. What should the pastor say? Write a precise statement defining success for a missionary.

. . . .
. . . .
. . . .
. . . .
. . . .

B. Discuss the concept of supporting nationals and decide what your church will do.

   ....
   ....
   ....
   ....
   ....

C. Discuss the concept of "partnering" and decide what your church will do.

   ....
   ....
   ....
   ....
   ....

the church should not try to micromanage how the missionary should do his job

7 AGENCIES

Many churches choose to use the services of a mission agency. There are a wide variety of them, and churches would do well to vet them and use the agencies that are best suited for them and the missionary. The assumption is that the local church should be in the driver's seat of missions, and thus it is worth your effort to wrestle with the issues related to sending agencies.

A. Determine whether or not you want to use **Clearing House** or **Full Service** agencies to send missionaries.

___ Clearing House because

....
....
....

___ Full Service because

....
....
....

B. Make a list of services you will provide for a missionary you send, regardless of whether or not they join a mission agency.

   ....
   ....
   ....
   ....
   ....
   ....
   ....
   ....
   ....
   ....
   ....
   ....
   ....
   ....
   ....

C. Make a list of the things that are important to your church when choosing a mission agency.

   ....
   ....
   ....
   ....
   ....
   ....
   ....

D. Make a list of agencies your church will use. This will take thorough research that cannot be completed in this group meeting. The first step is to identify the agencies you would like to vet and then assign a team to do the research, based on criteria that are important to your church.

....

....

....

....

....

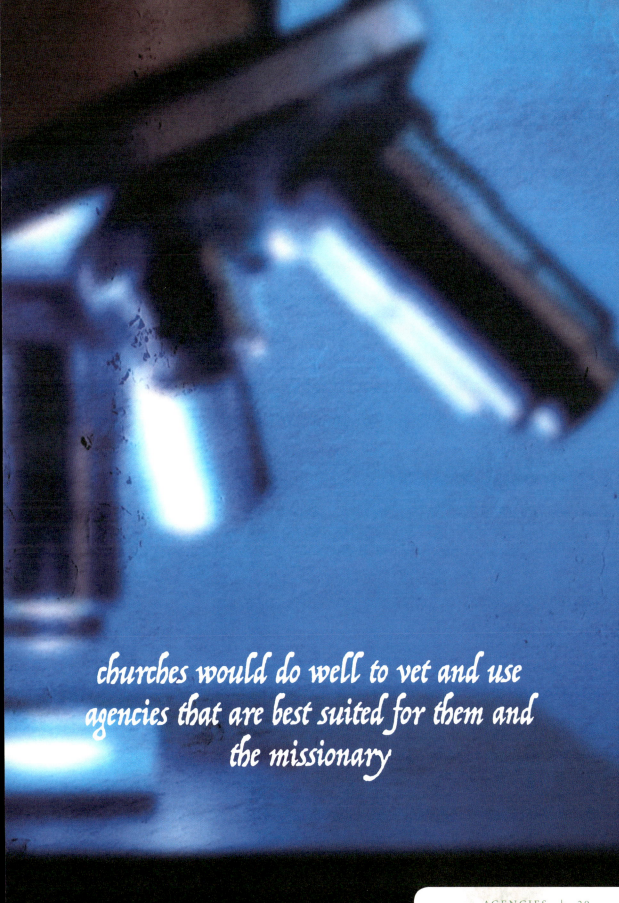

churches would do well to vet and use agencies that are best suited for them and the missionary

8 MONEY

Ultimately, the discussion about missions will touch on the topic of how to fund the endeavor. The leadership of a church would do well to carefully think through the issues of finances and come to a consensus about how they will view this topic. This session will help crystalize some thinking about how to finance Great Commission ministries.

A. Does your church want to do anything to help new missionaries deal with school debt? If "yes" then what?

   ....
   ....
   ....
   ....
   ....

B. What is your church's position on **Faith Promise**.

   ....
   ....
   ....

C. Discuss your church's position on missionaries raising support from individuals (in addition to or rather than churches).

D. What is your church's position related to alternate approaches for funding missions like **Tentmaking** and **BAM**?

What is your approach to helping your missionaries raise their support?

9 PRAYER

Not many would denigrate the importance of prayer in missions, but there are not many who faithfully, fervently pray in a biblical manner for the missionaries they send. There tends to be a hit-or-miss approach to sustaining missionaries by prayer. One critical component to Great Commission ministries in your church is to have a well-thought-out strategy for prayer.

A. What will be your church's prayer commitment to missionaries?

   ....
   ....
   ....
   ....
   ....

B. What will be your church's prayer strategy for missionaries?

   ....
   ....
   ....

....
....
....
....
....
....
....
....

C. What will your church do to propagate the 7 biblical prayer requests for missionaries on an ongoing basis to the congregation?

....
....
....
....
....

D. Who is the point person to be the prayer cheerleader for missions in your church?

....

there are not many who faithfully, fervently pray in a biblical manner for the missionaries they send

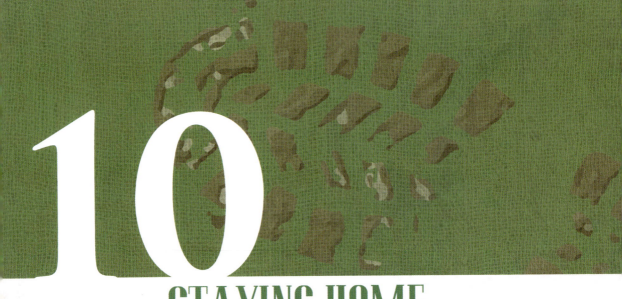

10
STAYING HOME

A. List all the strategies your church has for supporting missionaries from other churches. What does *propempo* look like in your church?

B. List all the strategies your church has for supporting your own missionaries. What does *propempo* look like in your church?

....
....
....
....
....
....
....
....
....
....
....
....
....

C. Establish a strategy for helping the sending church realize their importance in the missionary endeavor.

....
....
....
....
....
....
....
....
....
....
....
....

What is your strategy to learning and improving your church by learning from the experience and expertise of missionaries?

....
....
....
....
....
....
....
....
....
....
....

sending and staying should be mutually beneficial

CONCLUSION

Make a list of 50 things your church can do to make sure a first-time visitor knows without any doubt that your church is involved in the Great Commission.

1. ....
2. ....
3. ....
4. ....
5. ....
6. ....
7. ....
8. ....
9. ....
10. ....

11. ....
12. ....
13. ....
14. ....
15. ....
16. ....
17. ....
18. ....
19. ....
20. ....
21. ....
22. ....
23. ....
24. ....
25. ....
26. ....
27. ....
28. ....
29. ....
30. ....
31. ....
32. ....
33. ....
34. ....
35. ....
36. ....
37. ....

38. ....
39. ....
40. ....
41. ....
42. ....
43. ....
44. ....
45. ....
46. ....
47. ....
48. ....
49. ....
50. ....

what can you do to show that your church is involved in the Great Commission?

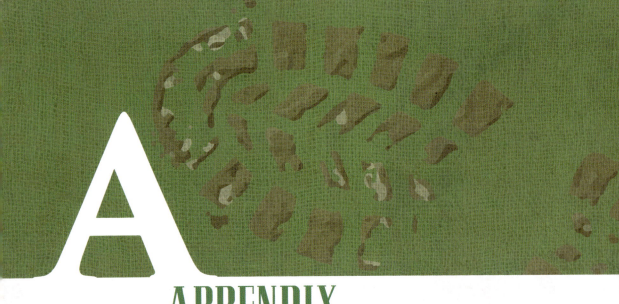

APPENDIX

OUTCOME OBJECTIVES FOR AN EQUIPPED LEADER

How can church leaders know whether a man is ready to begin pastoring? What attributes, abilities, and experiences should he have before being ordained for ministry?" The list below, created by church-planting missionaries in South Africa, incorporates not only the biblical character mandates, but the knowledge, skills, and basic experiences a person should have to be ordained to minister as an elder, pastor, or missionary.

Review the list. In the second column, write a number from 1 (least) to 5 (best) of your preparedness in that area.

OUTCOME OBJECTIVES ATTRIBUTES, ABILITIES, AND EXPERIENCES	1-5
FAMILY	
His marriage, family, work, and personal life are God-pleasing, consistent, integrated, and balanced.	
He is a godly leader of his wife and children.	

OUTCOME OBJECTIVES
ATTRIBUTES, ABILITIES, AND EXPERIENCES

FAMILY *(cont.)*

His wife has some level of formal education and has received personal mentoring.

His wife is supportive of him training in the church-based program and of his future ministry.

Their children, if still at home, live an orderly life, not given to open rebellion or immoral conduct.

He and his wife are both hospitable and share what God has provided for them.

He and his wife understand the public nature of pastoral ministry, guidelines for alleviating the pressures it can have on a pastor's family, etc.

He is family-oriented in his affections and scheduling and not given to overworking.

Finances. He can live on a budget, pays bills on time, and is not in debt (except for appreciable items such as a house).

CHARACTER

He has a high and biblical view of God, Christ, and the Scripture.

He is oriented to Scripture-based priorities, planning, and problem resolution.

He understands his personality, strengths, giftedness, weaknesses, and tendencies.

He has a serious and appropriate view of self and is committed to life-long learning.

He has a love of people and can balance the demands of tasks and people.

He evidences the manifestation of the fruit and gifts of one filled with the Word and the Holy Spirit.

He has an eager desire to serve as a leader (deacon, elder, or pastor).

He is blameless and above reproach; he has a "Teflon life" (no accusation hurled at him will stick).

OUTCOME OBJECTIVES
ATTRIBUTES, ABILITIES, AND EXPERIENCES

1-5

CHARACTER (cont.)

He has a good reputation with people in the marketplace, at work, at school, etc.	
He is temperate and self-controlled.	
He is generally self-disciplined in his habits of eating, driving, TV viewing, sports/hobbies, budgeting, etc.	
Although he may have a sense of humor, he is generally a serious person and thinks honestly about himself and others close to him.	
He has good behavior and will apologize when he has engaged in wrong or questionable conduct.	
He must be honest and be a man of his word; he mustn't promise too hastily or be double-tongued.	
He is not given to wine or other addictive substances.	
He is not violent in speech, gestures, or actions.	
He is not greedy for money and does not gamble or partake in schemes to get money without working suitably for it.	
He responds biblically when corrected and looks for truth in any criticism.	
He responds biblically when offended/wronged.	
He invites periodic, positive criticism of his ministry by his leadership.	
He responds appropriately to changes in circumstances.	
He is a team player when set among other leaders and is not quarrelsome or autocratic.	
He understands that ministry is "people work" and has good people skills.	
He has a meek and gentle spirit.	
He understands that leadership means serving others.	
He finishes tasks undertaken correctly and on time unless properly delegated.	

OUTCOME OBJECTIVES
ATTRIBUTES, ABILITIES, AND EXPERIENCES

1-5

CHARACTER *(cont.)*

He can keep a confidence.

He has a daily devotional life and is committed to regular study of God's Word.

He diligently keeps a clear conscience before the Lord and others and is quick to confess, repent, and forsake a known sin.

He does not covet positions and is not overly ambitious.

He understands and has demonstrated the value of time management, punctuality, and scheduling.

He keeps a personal book containing a daily log of activities, appointments, schedules, calendars, addresses, and phone numbers, etc.

He manages his time well.

He understands the principles of biblical decision-making.

He has established and updated short-, medium-, and long-term goals and understands strategic planning.

He has an understanding of priorities and conflicting interests and can say no to good things.

CHURCH-RELATED SKILLS - PASTORING

He is fully prepared for ordination.

He is committed to having a deep prayer life.

He has a good grasp of shepherding—leading, feeding, comforting, and protecting the flock.

He knows how to provide meaningful comfort and practical help to those who are grieving.

He understands the different leadership styles, giftedness, and temperament types of people that he ministers with and to.

He has thought through and developed a written philosophy of ministry.

OUTCOME OBJECTIVES
ATTRIBUTES, ABILITIES, AND EXPERIENCES

CHURCH-RELATED SKILLS - PASTORING *(cont.)*

He has demonstrated the ability to interact and work well with other church leaders on various levels.

He is familiar with biblical and popular methods of church growth and their strengths and weaknesses.

He is familiar with church structure concepts such as cell or growth groups, discipleship networks, etc.

He has a biblical position on major social issues.

He knows how to apply Scripture practically to the situations of life.

CHURCH-RELATED SKILLS - PULPIT MINISTRY

He is committed to regular study of the Word and has sound exegetical skills.

He can communicate effectively God's truth either one-on-one or to a group.

He can present the Word in both topical and expository formats and knows the pros and cons of both.

He knows the methods and guidelines for conducting weddings and funerals and infant dedications.

He has experience in conducting the Lord's Table and baptisms.

CHURCH-RELATED SKILLS - EVANGELISM

He evangelizes along the way and actively builds relationships with unbelievers.

He is familiar with different evangelistic styles, i.e., testimonial, confrontational, etc.

He can make smooth transitions to spiritual topics.

He is familiar with evangelism training courses.

OUTCOME OBJECTIVES
ATTRIBUTES, ABILITIES, AND EXPERIENCES

CHURCH-RELATED SKILLS - EVANGELISM *(cont.)*

He is familiar with various evangelism methods such as street, puppet, and musical evangelism, etc.

He is familiar with the needs of the culture or community in which he evangelizes.

CHURCH-RELATED SKILLS - COUNSELING

He is familiar with the principles of biblical counseling, confidentiality, accountability, etc.

He is generally familiar with popular but unbiblical philosophies and psychologies and can explain the differences.

He knows how to apply Scripture practically to the situations of life in counseling.

He understands the value of, and guidelines for, in-home visits of visitors and church families.

He understands the value of, and guidelines for, visiting the sick.

He understands the value of, and guidelines for, encouragement of families of the sick or deceased.

CHURCH-RELATED SKILLS - DEACON & ELDER

He meets the biblical qualifications for an elder or deacon.

He has learned mediation and conflict-resolution skills.

He is able to confront graciously and in a supportive, pro-active manner.

He is familiar with the pros and cons of various models of church governance and has a preferred model supported by the Scripture.

He is thoroughly acquainted with the guidelines and procedures involved in church discipline of leaders and church members and its possible repercussions.

He can recognize men suitable for church leadership and can recognize unqualified persons.

OUTCOME OBJECTIVES
ATTRIBUTES, ABILITIES, AND EXPERIENCES
1-5

CHURCH-RELATED SKILLS - DISCIPLESHIP

He understands the importance of having a discipleship ministry with other young men, and he can and has discipled other believers.	
He fully understands the concept of church-based leadership development.	
He understands the importance of training men who give families and the church stability and leadership.	
He is familiar with biblical passages on discipleship and the different models of discipleship.	

CHURCH-RELATED SKILLS - ADMINISTRATION

He can administer a church's ministries and office.	
He is willing to delegate to those who may not do the job as well as he can.	
He understands the balance between keeping a schedule and keeping flexible.	
He understands basic organizational accounting.	
He can organize and manage personnel, volunteers, and paid staff.	
He knows who and where his administrative and service resources are.	
He understands that the Constitution and By-Laws are a limitation on the exercise of arbitrary authority, and that they bind him to certain requirements and procedures in the running of the church.	

CHURCH-RELATED SKILLS - MISSIONS

He understands the global responsibilities of his local church in reproducing church-planting churches here and abroad.	
He understands how regular and periodic missions giving fits into a church's budget.	
He is thoroughly acquainted with the church planting process and the various models of church planting.	

OUTCOME OBJECTIVES
ATTRIBUTES, ABILITIES, AND EXPERIENCES

CHURCH-RELATED SKILLS - MISSIONS *(cont.)*

He understands the virtues of a good missions program and policy and the characteristics of a poor one.

CHURCH-RELATED SKILLS - ADULT EDUCATION

He is familiar with general teaching methods, course preparation, text selection, lesson plans, class decorum, and teaching skills.

He is familiar with the differences between preaching and teaching and knows how to adjust his teaching to the level of his students.

He has designed and taught a church-based education course.

CHURCH-RELATED SKILLS - USHERING

He can schedule and administer an ushering/greeting staff.

He is familiar with the use and storage of various forms of church literature such as bulletins, brochures, visitors' cards, tracts, display tables, sign-up sheets, etc.

He has experience in greeting, seating, and taking offerings.

He understands the importance of first impressions of visitors, and the vital role of the usher.

CHURCH-RELATED SKILLS - MUSIC MINISTRY

He can lead singing and choose music for a church service.

He knows biblical principles concerning music, what is unbiblical, what is preference, and how to deal with other music issues using scriptural doctrine for this dispensation.

CHURCH-RELATED SKILLS - SUNDAY SCHOOL

He can design a Sunday School curriculum plan for pre-school through high school age groups.

He can design a series of lessons with lesson plans appropriate to each age group.

OUTCOME OBJECTIVES
ATTRIBUTES, ABILITIES, AND EXPERIENCES

CHURCH-RELATED SKILLS - SUNDAY SCHOOL (cont.)

He can capably use media in teaching.	
He has a basic knowledge of available Sunday School curricula.	
He can train and assist others in developing lesson plans.	

CHURCH-RELATED SKILLS - YOUTH MINISTRIES

He is able to design and implement a youth program for Grades 1 through 12.	
He is familiar with resources for youth programs.	
He is familiar with guidelines for running a youth program, both as to education and activities.	

CHURCH-RELATED SKILLS - LADIES MINISTRY

He can teach an appropriate ladies' study, course, or Sunday school.	
He is familiar with the differences and dangers of working with and counseling women.	
His wife (if he is married) is able to capably lead a ladies' Bible study.	

CHURCH-RELATED SKILLS - NURSERY

He can organize a nursery ministry.	
He can capably and creatively work in a nursery.	
He can schedule and motivate nursery personnel.	
He can order and oversee supplies for nursery such as snacks, drinks, diapers, toys, fans, heaters, etc.	

OUTCOME OBJECTIVES
ATTRIBUTES, ABILITIES, AND EXPERIENCES

1-5

INTERPERSONAL SKILLS (see also Character, p.43)

He is conversant and shows a genuine interest in people.

He demonstrates the skill of encouragement.

He mixes and interacts well with people.

He is aware of his people- or task- orientation and is able to keep a proper balance between the two.

He is aware of cultural differences between people groups due to class, race, ethnicity, background, location, national history, etc., and he adapts well to differing classes and cultures.

He has a slightly higher than societal average ability to use the language in which he ministers.

He is not overly opinionated, is careful about stating opinion as fact, is not threatened by opposing opinions and does not make excessive reference to self in conversations.

COGNITIVE SKILLS

He can think critically and analytically.

He can follow detailed reasoning fairly well.

He knows why he believes what he believes and can support his views with Scripture.

He knows the differences between conviction and preference and between what is biblical and what is cultural.

He desires to be a life-long student and has demonstrated the habit of personal study.

He can recognize trends in society and predict consequences.

He knows where and who his academic and theological resources are for research and self-improvement.

OUTCOME OBJECTIVES
ATTRIBUTES, ABILITIES, AND EXPERIENCES

1-5

COMMUNICATION SKILLS *(see also Pulpit Ministry, p.46)*

He clearly communicates ideas in writing.	
He has a good working knowledge of grammar, vocabulary, and punctuation.	
He understands that different contexts demand differing use of writing styles.	
He has good reading comprehension and speed.	

BIBLE & THEOLOGICAL KNOWLEDGE

The Scripture is the final authority in his life and teaching and ministry.	
He has a good working knowledge of the Scripture.	
He is familiar with the themes, major divisions, authors, dates, and contexts of every book of the Bible and can explain how each gives us a picture of Christ.	
He can explain the significance of key New and Old Testament passages.	
He has memorized at least 200 verses of Scripture.	
He has taught at least 3 Old Testament books and 3 New Testament books to adult audiences.	
He is able to exegete and interpret the Scriptures literally, grammatically, and historically for use in sermons, teaching, and discipleship.	
He has prepared and given at least 50 different sermons.	
He has a working knowledge of Theology (Systematic, Biblical and Historical).	
He is familiar with the span of Church History and the major heresies and reformation movements.	
He is familiar with the religions, cults, and "isms" of the last two centuries and can detect and refute false teaching, error, and wrong doctrine.	

OUTCOME OBJECTIVES
ATTRIBUTES, ABILITIES, AND EXPERIENCES

1-5

BIBLE & THEOLOGICAL KNOWLEDGE (cont.)

He is familiar with the alphabet and basic nouns and verbs of Greek and Hebrew and knows how to use original language tools. Even with these, he must confess that he is under-equipped to use the original languages effectively and accurately.

He is very familiar with and has used research tools such as commentaries, Bible and theological dictionaries, interlinear texts, lexicons, etc.

He operates with an understanding of the different levels of dogmatism; i.e., the difference between speculation, opinion, supported belief, and convictions.

PERSONAL SKILLS

He has a language aptitude for any foreign language in which he hopes to minister.

He is computer literate, with good abilities in word processing and desktop publishing.

He understands the principles of professional dress.

PRACTICAL MINISTRY TOOLS

If technologically and financially feasible, he uses appropriate and current technology for communication.

He has access to at least one good set of conservative commentaries.

He has study tools such as concordances, an inter-linear text, Bible dictionaries, and theological dictionaries.

He has at least five different English versions of the Bible.

He has at least three books dealing with the history of the church.

He has a systematic theology text.

He has at least three apologetics books.

He has at least ten books on marriage, the family, raising of children, etc.

APPENDIX A | 53

OUTCOME OBJECTIVES FOR A LEADING LADY

Titus 2 makes it clear that women are to train women. But what does a fully trained lady look like? What is the profile of a woman who is fully equipped to impact the lives of others? The following is an inventory to help develop some goals for training.

Review the list. In the second column, write a number from 1 (least) to 5 (best) of your preparedness in that area.

OUTCOME OBJECTIVES — ATTRIBUTES, ABILITIES, AND EXPERIENCES	1-5
FAMILY	
Her marriage is God-pleasing, consistent, integrated, and balanced.	
Her family is God-pleasing, consistent, integrated and balanced.	
Her work is God-pleasing, consistent, integrated, and balanced.	
Her personal life is God-pleasing, consistent, integrated, and balanced.	
She influences others toward godliness.	
She has received personal mentoring.	
Her children, if still at home, live an orderly life, not given to open rebellion or immoral conduct.	
She is hospitable and shares what God has provided.	
She understands the public nature of pastoral ministry, guidelines for alleviating the pressures it can have on a pastor's family, etc.	
She is family-oriented in her affections and scheduling and not given to overworking.	
Finances. She can live on a budget, pays bills on time, and is not in debt (except for appreciable items such as a house).	

OUTCOME OBJECTIVES
ATTRIBUTES, ABILITIES, AND EXPERIENCES

1-5

FAMILY (cont.)

She pays attention to personal grooming and modesty.

CHARACTER

She has a high and biblical view of God, Christ, and the Scripture.

She is oriented to Scripture-based priorities.

She understands her personality, strengths, and giftedness.

She understands her personality, weaknesses, and tendencies.

She has a serious and appropriate view of self and is committed to life-long learning.

She has a love of people and can balance the demands of tasks and people.

She evidences the manifestation of the fruit and gifts of one filled with the Word and the Holy Spirit.

She has a willing desire to serve as a leader.

She is blameless and above reproach; she has a "Teflon life" (no accusation hurled at her will stick).

She has a good reputation with people in the marketplace, at work, at school, etc.

She is temperate and self-controlled.

She is generally self-disciplined in her habits of eating, driving, TV viewing, sports/hobbies, budgeting, etc.

Although she may have a sense of humor, she is generally a serious person and thinks honestly about herself and others close to her.

She has good behavior and will apologize when she has engaged in wrong or questionable conduct.

She is honest and a person of her word; doesn't promise too hastily or is double-tongued.

OUTCOME OBJECTIVES
ATTRIBUTES, ABILITIES, AND EXPERIENCES

CHARACTER *(cont.)*

She is not controlled by alcohol or other addictive substances.	
She is not violent in speech, gestures, or actions.	
She is not greedy for money or partakes in schemes to get money without working suitably for it.	
She responds biblically when corrected and looks for truth in any criticism.	
She is faithful in "little things."	
She responds biblically when offended/wronged.	
She invites periodic positive criticism of her ministry.	
She is a team player when set among other leaders and is not quarrelsome or autocratic.	
She understands that ministry is "people work" and has good people skills.	
She has a meek and gentle spirit.	
She understands that leadership means serving others.	
She finishes tasks undertaken correctly and on time unless properly delegated.	
She can keep a confidence.	
She has a daily devotional life and is committed to regular study of God's Word.	
She diligently keeps a clear conscience before the Lord and others and is quick to confess, repent, and forsake a known sin.	
She does not covet positions and is not overly ambitious.	
She understands and has demonstrated the value of time management, punctuality, and scheduling.	
She keeps a personal book containing a daily log of activities, appointments, schedules, calendars, addresses, and phone numbers, etc.	

OUTCOME OBJECTIVES
ATTRIBUTES, ABILITIES, AND EXPERIENCES

1-5

CHARACTER *(cont.)*

She manages her time well.

She understands the principles of biblical decision-making.

She has established and updated short-, medium-, and long-term goals and understands strategic planning.

She has an understanding of priorities and conflicting interests and can say no to good things.

CHURCH-RELATED SKILLS - MENTORING

She has discipled a new believer.

She is committed to having a deep prayer life.

She has a good grasp of concepts of mentoring.

She knows how to provide meaningful comfort and practical help to those who are grieving.

She understands the different leadership styles, giftedness, and temperament types of people that she ministers with and to.

She has thought through and developed a written philosophy of ministry.

She has demonstrated the ability to interact and work well with other leaders on various levels.

She has the people skills to relate to different kinds of people.

She is familiar with church structure concepts such as cell or growth groups, discipleship networks, etc.

She understands the balance of focusing on a few while ministering to many.

She has a biblical position on major social issues.

She knows how to apply Scripture practically to the situations of life.

OUTCOME OBJECTIVES
ATTRIBUTES, ABILITIES, AND EXPERIENCES

CHURCH-RELATED SKILLS - TEACHING MINISTRY

She is committed to regular study of the Word.	
She has sound exegetical skills.	
She can effectively communicate God's truth either one-on-one or to a group.	
She can present the Word in a systematic way so that people understand the text.	
She can conduct a ladies' Bible study.	
She can facilitate a Bible study discussion group.	

CHURCH-RELATED SKILLS - EVANGELISM

She evangelizes along the way and actively builds relationships with unbelievers.	
She is familiar with different evangelistic styles, i.e., testimonial, confrontational, etc.	
She can make smooth transitions to spiritual topics.	
She has led another person to Christ.	
She is familiar with various stages of evangelism.	
She is familiar with the needs of the culture or community in which she evangelizes.	

CHURCH-RELATED SKILLS - COUNSELING

She is familiar with the principles of biblical counseling, confidentiality, accountability, etc.	
She is generally familiar with popular but unbiblical philosophies and psychologies.	

OUTCOME OBJECTIVES
ATTRIBUTES, ABILITIES, AND EXPERIENCES

CHURCH-RELATED SKILLS - COUNSELING (cont.)

She knows how to apply Scripture practically to the situations of life in counseling.

She understands the value of, and guidelines for, in-home visits of visitors and church families.

She understands the value of, and guidelines for, visiting the sick.

She understands the value of, and guidelines for, encouragement of families of the sick or deceased.

CHURCH-RELATED SKILLS - LEADERSHIP

She meets the biblical qualifications of a Titus 2 woman.

She has learned mediation and conflict-resolution skills.

She is able to confront graciously and in a supportive, pro-active manner.

She understands the principles of servant leadership.

She has a high level of ambiguity tolerance.

She has a plan of life-long learning and self-improvement.

She can recognize others who have potential for leadership.

CHURCH-RELATED SKILLS - DISCIPLESHIP

She understands the importance of having a discipleship ministry with other young ladies.

She fully understands the concept of church-based leadership development.

She understands the importance of training women who give families and the church stability.

She is familiar with biblical passages on discipleship and the different models of discipleship.

OUTCOME OBJECTIVES
ATTRIBUTES, ABILITIES, AND EXPERIENCES

1-5

CHURCH-RELATED SKILLS - ADMINISTRATION

She can organize special events.	
She is willing to delegate to those who may not do the job as well as she can.	
She understands the balance between keeping a schedule and keeping flexible.	
She can organize and manage personnel, volunteers, and paid staff.	
She knows who and where her administrative and service resources are.	
She knows how to manage a household.	
She knows how to manage a project and keep within budget.	
She has secretarial skills (i.e. church calendars, newsletters, etc.)	

CHURCH-RELATED SKILLS - MISSIONS

She understands the global responsibilities of her local church in reproducing church-planting churches here and abroad.	
She understands the virtues of a good missions program and policy, and the characteristics of a poor one.	
She has gone on a missions trip.	
She knows how to practically and creatively minister to missionaries.	
She understands how regular and periodic missions giving fits into a church's budget.	
She is thoroughly acquainted with the church planting process and the various models of church planting.	
She demonstrates a heart for the missionary and her mission field.	
She is able to pass on information to the church that keeps people informed of the missionary's needs.	
She can effectively help develop and organize a missions conference.	

OUTCOME OBJECTIVES
ATTRIBUTES, ABILITIES, AND EXPERIENCES

1-5

CHURCH-RELATED SKILLS - ADULT EDUCATION

She is familiar with general teaching methods, course preparation, text selection, lesson plans, class decorum, and teaching skills.

She knows how to adjust her teaching to the level of her students.

She has designed and taught an adult education course.

CHURCH-RELATED SKILLS - HOSPITALITY

She has a desire to deepen her relationship with people through hospitality.

She has the cooking skills to provide attractive meals for visitors.

She understands the importance of first impressions of visitors, and the vital role of making visitors welcome to her home or church meetings.

CHURCH-RELATED SKILLS - SUNDAY SCHOOL

She can design a series of lessons with lesson plans appropriate to each age group.

She can capably use media in teaching.

She has a basic knowledge of available Sunday School curricula.

She can train and assist others in developing lesson plans and learning to teach.

She is capable of maintaining discipline in a classroom.

She understands characteristics of different age groups.

CHURCH-RELATED SKILLS - LADIES MINISTRY

She can teach an appropriate ladies' study, course, or Sunday School.

She is familiar with the differences and dangers of working with and counseling men.

She is able to capably lead a ladies' Bible study.

OUTCOME OBJECTIVES
ATTRIBUTES, ABILITIES, AND EXPERIENCES

CHURCH-RELATED SKILLS - NURSERY

She can organize a nursery ministry.	
She can capably and creatively work in a nursery.	
She can schedule and motivate nursery personnel.	
She can order and oversee supplies for nursery such as snacks, drinks, diapers, toys, fans, heaters, etc.	

INTERPERSONAL SKILLS *(see also Character, p.55)*

She is conversant and shows a genuine interest in people.	
She demonstrates the skill of encouragement.	
She mixes and interacts well with people.	
She is aware of her people- or task-orientation, and is able to keep a proper balance between the two.	
She is not overly opinionated and is careful about stating opinion as fact.	
She is not threatened by opposing opinions.	
She does not make excessive reference to self in conversations.	
She is aware of cultural differences between people groups due to class, race, ethnicity, background, location, national history, etc., and she adapts well to different cultures.	
She has a slightly higher than societal average ability to use the language in which she works.	

COGNITIVE SKILLS

She can think critically and analytically.	
She can follow detailed reasoning fairly well.	
She knows why she believes what she believes and can support her views with Scripture.	

OUTCOME OBJECTIVES
ATTRIBUTES, ABILITIES, AND EXPERIENCES

COGNITIVE SKILLS (cont.)

She knows the differences between conviction and preference and between what is biblical and what is cultural.

She desires to be a life-long student and has demonstrated the habit of personal study.

She can recognize trends in society and predict consequences.

She knows where and who her academic and theological resources are for research and self-improvement.

COMMUNICATION SKILLS

She clearly communicates ideas in writing.

She has a good working knowledge of grammar, vocabulary, and punctuation.

She understands that different contexts demand differing use of writing styles.

She has good reading comprehension and speed.

BIBLE & THEOLOGICAL KNOWLEDGE

The Scripture is the final authority in her life and teaching and ministry.

She has attended classroom learning sessions.

She has a good working knowledge of the Scripture.

She is familiar with the themes, major divisions, authors, dates, and contexts of every book of the Bible and can explain how each gives us a picture of Christ.

She can explain the significance of key New and Old Testament passages.

She has memorized at least 200 verses of Scripture.

She is able to exegete and interpret the Scriptures literally, grammatically, and historically for use in teaching and discipleship.

OUTCOME OBJECTIVES
ATTRIBUTES, ABILITIES, AND EXPERIENCES

BIBLE & THEOLOGICAL KNOWLEDGE (cont.)

She has prepared and given at least 50 different lessons.	
She has a working knowledge of Theology (Systematic, Biblical, and Historical).	
She is familiar with the religions, cults, and "isms" of the last two centuries and can detect and refute false teaching, error, and wrong doctrine.	
She is very familiar with and has used research tools such as commentaries, Bible and theological dictionaries, interlinear texts, lexicons, etc.	

PERSONAL SKILLS

She has a language aptitude for any foreign language in which she hopes to minister.	
She is computer literate, with good abilities in word processing and desktop publishing.	
She understands the principles of professional dress.	

PRACTICAL MINISTRY TOOLS

If technologically and financially feasible, she uses appropriate and current technology for communication.	
She has access to at least one good set of conservative commentaries.	
She has at least five different English versions of the Bible.	
She has a systematic theology text.	
She has at least ten books on marriage, the family, raising of children, etc.	
She has a least one book on apologetics.	

Made in the USA
Charleston, SC
13 April 2016